BOLD
CRAZY
& Faith 2

The MEDITATIONS

BOLD & CRAZY Faith 2

The MEDITATIONS

BEST SELLING AUTHOR

Daryn Carl Ramsey

Diamond & Light Publishing, LLC

Requests for information should be addressed to: darynramsey@ diamondandlight.com

Published by:
Diamond & Light Publishing, LLC, Belcamp, MD 21017

30 RELEVANT WAYS

TO LIVE BY FAITH TODAY: BOOK TWO

BOLD & CRAZY Faith 2
The MEDITATIONS

BEST-SELLING AUTHOR
Daryn Carl Ramsey

CONTENTS

DEDICATION

I want to dedicate this project to my loving and beautiful wife, Deborah, who has been a major blessing in my life. We have both dedicated our lives to God, family, and each other for so many years, and as a result, we have received supernatural favor. You have been by my side as we have enjoyed the experience of mountain highs and endured valley lows living and leaning on God together. Truly, "He who finds a wife finds a good thing, And obtains favor from the Lord" (Proverbs 18:22 NKJV). Deb, I respect, cherish, and love you dearly!

I also dedicate this project to my loving parents, the late Carl and Arlene Ramsey. I love, miss, and think about you both every day. I am grateful for your love and thank you for everything you did for me. Also, I want to dedicate this project to my entire family. I love and appreciate you all.

Thank you to my Lord and Savior, Jesus Christ!

Had it not been for you on my side, where would I be? Lord, you are spectacular! Heavenly Father, thank you for the mission that you gave me to talk to your people and teach them about faith. Now I understand why you were so persistent and adamant about the mission. Got it! As you lead and I follow, lives will continue to be changed. Thank you for your persistence. Once again, I dedicate this book and my life to you.

ACKNOWLEDGMENTS

I want to thank my wife, Deb, who is a major factor in the most important decisions I make in my life. Having Deb's support for Bold & Crazy Faith 2 in the same way as the first book is truly a blessing. We do our best to support each other in all our endeavors, individually and collectively, and make a wonderful team. I want to thank my mentor, award-winning publisher, and filmmaker Tressa Azarel Smallwood, who has been an inspiration and driving force for me to create content and intellectual property that will pay dividends in the short and long term.

I also want to thank all my business associates and interns, who have assisted in the publishing of this work. Thank you to my alma mater Virginia State University, VSU Alumni Association-Baltimore Chapter, VSU Prayer Warriors, and Moderators for your continued support. To all my followers on social media and readers of my blog and books, thank you from the bottom of my heart. Without you, this project could not happen. Finally, a special thank you to God, who has been the unwavering force in my life. Heavenly Father, you have been there for me through my darkest hours and in my greatest experiences. My God! Thank you! Once again, I dedicate this book to You, and You already know that I have dedicated my life to You.

INTRODUCTION

I authored this book to help believers increase their faith and make an immediate impact on people around the world. In today's culture of microwave mentalities and a climate of high anxiety, uncertainty, and dwindling hope, I felt a need to pen and publish a work that will provide faith to the masses right now. Due mostly to the unprecedented and ongoing pandemic and volatile political practices we have endured, a powerful injection of faith is just what the chief physician (God) has ordered to offer resolve to the needs of this society at this time. Bold & Crazy Faith 2: The Meditations will provide thirty relevant ways to live by faith today!

This book was created to encourage you to connect with God daily and designed to be highly impactful immediately. Bold & Crazy Faith 2 is comprehensive, offering a variety of applicable techniques to build and sustain your faith, improve your relationship with God, and increase the quality of your life significantly. Make no mistake about it—this book is life changing. As you read the daily meditations and adopt and apply them to your life, a transformation will take place as you commit and dedicate a brief period to this practice. God will meet you here, the place you have committed to meet Him regularly and form a more intimate relationship with Him. The Bible says, "But blessed are those who trust in the LORD and have made the LORD their hope and confidence" (Jeremiah 17:7 NLT).

Bold & Crazy Faith 2 is meant to be read multiple times. The meditations and scriptures will minister to you according to your specific needs and circumstances at that time and as God continues to guide. God will make himself available to you. His favor and guidance in your life are all you need to walk into your blessings. Choose God, for He has already chosen you. He is just waiting for you to acknowledge Him and turn to Him for His guidance and direction. Bold & Crazy Faith is knowing that you will live a victorious life because of your relationship as a child of God and your personal, intimate connection with Jesus Christ.

Bold & Crazy Faith 2 will motivate you to follow God's paths and not your own. Jesus said, "I am the way, the truth, and the life" (John

14:6 NIV). As you grow to trust in the Lord and the Lord knows that He can trust you, you will receive overflow. You just need to do the work. Similarly, as you become more focused and dedicated to your time with God, your time with Him can grow to be considered a labor of love. Focus and commitment are the keys to maximizing the effects of your meditations. So, will you be committed to implementing this beneficial technique to become a regular practice in your Christian lifestyle? Making this commitment will be one of the best decisions in your life. Be Bold and be Blessed in your reading and commitment to Bold & Crazy Faith 2: The Meditations!

DAY 1

Opening Your Mind

Education's purpose is to replace an empty mind with an open one.

—Malcolm Forbes
American Entrepreneur and Publisher of
Forbes Magazine

Today, you will willfully decide to believe God to work out issues in your life. Your mindset changes today. Make a note on your calendar to remind yourself that today was the day your mindset shifted to trust God for supernatural things in your life. Also, mark your calendar on the day God delivers and makes good on your prayer request. He will do it...oh yes, He will! Today is the day to set aside time and open your mind to building your **Faith**! You will benefit as your **Faith** increases. Today, you will do just that.

1

BOLD ACTIONS

_____

_____

_____

_____

_____

_____

_____

_____

_____

_____

_____

_____

_____

BOLD ACTIONS

_____

_____

_____

_____

_____

_____

_____

_____

_____

_____

_____

_____

BOLD ACTIONS

_____

_____

_____

_____

_____

_____

_____

_____

_____

_____

_____

_____

BOLD ACTIONS

_____

_____

_____

_____

_____

_____

_____

_____

_____

_____

_____

_____

BOLD ACTIONS

_____

_____

_____

_____

_____

_____

_____

_____

_____

_____

_____

DAY 2

Seeking God Early

*The first thing I do when I start my day is, I get
down on my hands and knees and give thanks to
God. Whenever I go outside of my house, the first
thing I do is stop at the church.*

—Mark Walberg
Academy Award Nominated Actor/Producer

When you seek God on a regular basis, you
will see your life change. One of my wife
Deb's favorite scriptures is Proverbs 8:17–21
(KJV), "I love them that love me; and those that
seek me early shall find me. Riches and honor
are with me, yea, durable riches, and righteousness. My fruit is better than gold, yea, than fine
gold, and my revenue than choice silver. I lead
in the way of righteousness, in the midst of the
paths of judgment: That I may cause those that
love me to inherit substance; and I will fill their

treasures." Whenever I hear or read these verses, I think about my wife one hundred percent of the time. I love her voice and how she sounds when she recites this verse. But not only do I think about her, I think of the simplicity, directness, and outcomes God provides as He advises those who love Him and seek Him.

God is saying, "Love me and I will reciprocate. Look for me and I will make myself available to you. Everything, including the honor that you need to give me, I already have. My ways are righteous.

Everything that I have to offer is better than even gold, and my worth is better than the best silver. I will teach, instruct, and provide righteous guidance. Love me and I will bless you with wonderful things of God, and I will bless you abundantly." Wow! If that is not enough inspiration to seek God today, then I need to work much harder to get you there.

Seek God early and you will find Him. Early means in the morning, now, or today. Seek God first and keep your mind focused on Him. Keep your heart fixed on God. When your heart and your mind are in the right place, good things will follow. Rewards, blessings, healing, production, and more will come when you seek God. But are you ready for my favorite one? **Peace**. Peace will also come when you seek God! As you seek God and receive His favor, your **Faith** will grow. If you are not seeking God on a regular basis, begin today. God will deliver! Trust Him.

BOLD ACTIONS

_____

_____

_____

_____

_____

_____

_____

_____

_____

_____

_____

_____

BOLD ACTIONS

_____

_____

_____

_____

_____

_____

_____

_____

_____

_____

_____

_____

BOLD ACTIONS

_____

_____

_____

_____

_____

_____

_____

_____

_____

_____

_____

BOLD ACTIONS

_____

_____

_____

_____

_____

_____

_____

_____

_____

_____

_____

_____

_____

BOLD ACTIONS

_____

_____

_____

_____

_____

_____

_____

_____

_____

_____

_____

_____

DAY 3

Studying God's Word

You need to be able to rain on all the seeds that are inside of you, and constantly nurture your potential that GOD placed inside of you by watering it with that WORD.

—LL Cool J
Rapper / Actor

God has given you all the tools that you need to thrive. One of the things He has given you to build your faith is study. Study His Word. To study God's Word is to take part in one of the most liberating and beneficial experiences that you can ever find. When you are depressed, the truth in God's Word will encourage, strengthen, and guide you. When you are seeking guidance about how to go about living your life, you can obtain that guidance from studying God's Word. If you need wisdom to deal with havoc in your life, the book of Proverbs is known for the wisdom it provides. If you are afraid about a situation, you are in or are about to enter today, study 2 Timothy 1:7 (NKJV) and learn, "For God has not given us a spirit of fear, but of power and of love and of a sound mind." God has given you His Word to share the gospel of Jesus Christ and provide the ultimate guidance to live your life according to how He desires you, His creation, to live. If God has given you the roadmap in His Word, why not study it to see where He wants you to go, what He wants you to do, and who He wants you to be.

BOLD ACTIONS

BOLD ACTIONS

_____

_____

_____

_____

_____

_____

_____

_____

_____

_____

_____

_____

BOLD ACTIONS

_____

_____

_____

_____

_____

_____

_____

_____

_____

_____

_____

_____

BOLD ACTIONS

_____

_____

_____

_____

_____

_____

_____

_____

_____

_____

_____

_____

DAY 4

Applying God's Word

I read from the Bible every day, and I read my Daily Word. I read something great yesterday. It said, "Don't aspire to make a living, aspire to make a difference."

—Denzel Washington
Academy Award-Winning Actor/Producer/
Director

What does it mean to apply the Word to your life? It means to do what the Word of God instructs you to do. Let the Word inspired by God guide you. "Do to others as you would have them do to you" (Luke 6:31 NIV). Put the golden rule into practice. Blessed are the peacemakers, so be the person who provides peace, and you will be blessed.

Apply the living Word of God to your life and

get tangible results. Always clap your hands and bless the Lord. Seek and knock. God's instructions not only tell you what to do but also how to put the plan into action. Do this, and this will be the result.

Sadly, so many people read but never even attempt to implement the guidance inspired by God or instruction from Jesus Christ. Imagine a firefighter trained to spray foam on a gas or grease fire who decides to disregard the instruction manual and spray water on the fire, making it intensify. Why would you do that if you have been given instruction, training, guidance, and inspiration? But I am here to tell you that God's Word is better than any instruction manual could ever be.

Be intentional today, tomorrow, and every day to read and apply the Word of God to your life, as you will learn that obedience is key to living a life full of peace and abundance.

BOLD ACTIONS

_____

_____

_____

_____

_____

_____

_____

_____

_____

_____

_____

_____

_____

BOLD ACTIONS

_____

_____

_____

_____

_____

_____

_____

_____

_____

_____

_____

_____

BOLD ACTIONS

_____

_____

_____

_____

_____

_____

_____

_____

_____

_____

_____

_____

BOLD ACTIONS

_____

_____

_____

_____

_____

_____

_____

_____

_____

_____

_____

DAY 5

Affirmations to Live By

You are fearless. You're not scared of anything.

—**Selena Gomez**
American Singer

Affirmations are an act of saying or showing that something is true. Build your faith by affirmations that motivate you to live out your victory in Christ! Proverbs 18:21 (MSG) says, "Words kill, words give life; they're either poison or fruit—you choose." So, choose words, sayings, and scriptures that build and inspire you and give you the confidence to win. Affirmations will help you have victory for yourself and for those entrusted in your care, whether it be family, friends, coworkers, or associates. Affirmations work best when they have a special meaning to you for personal or sentimental reasons. Plan to use affirmations every day of your life until they become something you just do without thinking about it.

Affirmations can be used at the start of your day to get you motivated, or affirmations can be used when you feel melancholy and need a spiritual pick-me-up. Let the truth in affirmations set you free. A powerful scripture to leverage as one of your affirmations can be found in Romans 8:28 (NIV), "And we know that in all things God works for the good of those that love him, who have been called according to his purpose." "Who is this King of Glory? The Lord strong and mighty, the Lord mighty in battle" (Psalms 24:8 NIV). He is the King of Kings who works for your good in all things. Knowing this is a fantastic way to start, spend, or finish your day!

BOLD ACTIONS

_____

_____

_____

_____

_____

_____

_____

_____

_____

_____

_____

_____

_____

BOLD ACTIONS

_____

_____

_____

_____

_____

_____

_____

_____

_____

_____

_____

BOLD ACTIONS

_____

_____

_____

_____

_____

_____

_____

_____

_____

_____

_____

_____

BOLD ACTIONS

_____

_____

_____

_____

_____

_____

_____

_____

_____

_____

_____

_____

_____

DAY 6

Acting on Your Faith

There's a scripture in the Book of James which says, Become a doer of the Word and not a hearer only. A hearer is someone who looks into a mirror, walks away, and quickly forgets what sort of person he is.

—Terrence Howard
American Actor

Having faith in God and yourself is great, but having faith means acting on it. Acting on your faith means your actions and the moves you make are attributed to your belief and relationship with God. Realizing who you are in Christ and all the benefits that come along with it should make acting on your faith second nature. As such, your actions in life should be bold with expectations of remarkable things.

Acts 4:13 (NLT) states, "The members of the council were amazed when they saw the boldness of Peter and John, for they could see that they were ordinary men with no special training in the Scriptures. They also recognized them as men who had been with Jesus." Have you ever decided to step out into something big and a little scary, but you had the full expectation that you would accomplish and complete what you set out to do? Well, just as Peter and John displayed their boldness because of their connection with Jesus, you can too. Trust God to help you accomplish something you have been thinking about for a long time. Remember, you need to move if you want to see the result. Decide to act on your faith today!

BOLD ACTIONS

_____

_____

_____

_____

_____

_____

_____

_____

_____

_____

_____

_____

BOLD ACTIONS

_____

_____

_____

_____

_____

_____

_____

_____

_____

_____

_____

_____

_____

BOLD ACTIONS

BOLD ACTIONS

_____

_____

_____

_____

_____

_____

_____

_____

_____

_____

_____

_____

_____

DAY 7

Journaling for Accountability

I have standards I don't plan on lowering for anybody... including myself.

—Zendaya
American Actress

Establish a journaling system where you can record your worries, concerns, troubles, or favorable expectations. Journaling your thoughts will help you be accountable to yourself and your circumstances. For most, writing provides an extra record besides what is filed in your memory. When things are written, you also have a better chance of acting on them to achieve results. As God works out and answers these worries, concerns, troubles, and expectations, record your outcomes. Over time, you will realize just how active God is in your life, and your faith will increase continually. He will answer, deliver, remove, fix, resolve, and bless you more than you recognize! That is fire right there!

BOLD ACTIONS

_____

_____

_____

_____

_____

_____

_____

_____

_____

_____

_____

_____

_____

_____

BOLD ACTIONS

_____

_____

_____

_____

_____

_____

_____

_____

_____

_____

_____

_____

BOLD ACTIONS

_____

_____

_____

_____

_____

_____

_____

_____

_____

_____

_____

_____

_____

BOLD ACTIONS

_____

_____

_____

_____

_____

_____

_____

_____

_____

_____

_____

DAY 8

Decreeing and Declaring God's Word

If you want to change the direction of your life,
change the declaration of your lips.

—Steven Furtick
Pastor, Songwriter, and New York Times
Best-Selling Author

One surefire way to build your faith and live a bold, abundant life is by decreeing and declaring God's Word. To decree means to make an official and authoritative order, especially one having the backing and reinforcement of law. To declare means to state something emphatically and announce officially. To declare God's Word is to proclaim that you agree with His Word as the truth. Your declaration displays your trust in God. Romans 1:16–17 (MSG) states, "It's news I'm most proud to proclaim, this extraordinary Message of God's powerful plan to rescue

45

everyone who trusts him, starting with Jews and then right on to everyone else! God's way of putting people right shows up in the acts of faith, confirming what Scripture has said all along: "The person in right standing before God by trusting him really lives."

Job 22:28 (KJV) states, "Thou shalt also decree a thing and it shall be established unto thee: and the light shall shine upon thy ways." To make a decree, you must be in a position of power and authority. As a Christian, you can do just that.

Luke 10:19 (NIV) states, "I have given you authority to trample on snakes and scorpions and to overcome all the power of the enemy; nothing will harm you." So now that you are armed with the wisdom to decree and declare the will of God, do so with the power, conviction, and authority your Heavenly Father has given you.

BOLD ACTIONS

_____

_____

_____

_____

_____

_____

_____

_____

_____

_____

_____

_____

BOLD ACTIONS

_____

_____

_____

_____

_____

_____

_____

_____

_____

_____

_____

BOLD ACTIONS

_____

_____

_____

_____

_____

_____

_____

_____

_____

_____

_____

_____

_____

BOLD ACTIONS

_____

_____

_____

_____

_____

_____

_____

_____

_____

_____

_____

_____

DAY 9

Memorizing Verses

*The Bible was and remains the biggest influ-
ence on my thinking. I was raised reading it,
memorizing passages from it, and being guided
by it. I still find it a source of wisdom, comfort,
and encouragement.*

—Hillary Clinton
United States Secretary of State
United States Senator
First Lady of the United States

How do you increase your faith so that you
can live a bold, meaningful, and prosper-
ous life in Christ? Memory verses are one way to
increase your faith. In the same way that you are
inspired, influenced, and motivated by the lyrics
to your favorite gospel hymns or songs, you will
also be inspired by memorizing relevant scriptures to increase or build your faith. Memorizing

verses from the Bible will allow the Word of God to have a lasting effect on your mind, soul, and spirit. When you already know what God has said about a circumstance or what you should do when you are confronted with a situation, you already have your resolution and answer.

Memorizing Bible verses is one of the most effective and easiest ways to equip and empower yourself as you continue to develop as a Christian. Memorize and call on the Word of God as you prepare to fight the fiery darts of the enemy trying to steal your joy and quench your thirst for righteousness. Memorize and call on Bible verses and make them personal to you and applicable to your situation. When people revolt against you, speak the words found in Psalms 91:4 (NJKV), "He shall cover you with His feathers, And under His wings you shall take refuge; His truth *shall be your* shield and buckler." Speak the words that you have memorized to give you boldness and encouragement to fulfill your desire to soar in life. Call on those memory verses that have been keeping you motivated from day to day. Make your impact in the world today. "Jesus Christ is the same yesterday and today and forever" (Hebrews 13:8 NIV).

BOLD ACTIONS

_____

_____

_____

_____

_____

_____

_____

_____

_____

_____

_____

_____

BOLD ACTIONS

_____

_____

_____

_____

_____

_____

_____

_____

_____

_____

_____

BOLD ACTIONS

_____

_____

_____

_____

_____

_____

_____

_____

_____

_____

_____

_____

_____

BOLD ACTIONS

_____

_____

_____

_____

_____

_____

_____

_____

_____

_____

_____

DAY 10

Leveraging Your Experiences

Best move I've ever made...Developed a deep relationship with Jesus Christ.

—Rev Run
Reverend/Legendary Rapper/Actor

Use your past experiences of how God brought you through as a key indicator that if He did it before, He will do it again. God is faithful and just. He did not bring you this far to leave you now. Build your faith from this. God does not bring you to a destination, drop you off, and leave you! No, no, no! God says, "I am with you!" We say, God with us! Oh yes, oh yes. Build from your knowledge of this. I am getting excited just writing this! Can you tell?

Use your past experiences with God to build your faith.

1. Leverage God's record of blessing you.
2. Use God's record of delivering you out of harm's way.
3. Leverage God's record of elevation in your life.

Now, meditate on these things!

To build your encouragement today, build on the knowledge that you have come this far by faith. This same faith will help you to prepare tables in the presence of your enemies, give Satan a black eye, and catapult you over every obstacle designed to stop you from walking in your purpose and affecting the lives of others. Your Bold & Crazy Faith will one day help you arrive at your destination and hear from your Almighty God, "Well done thou good and faithful servant" (Matthew 25:21 KJV). Now that should be enough inspiration to carry you through the year, nevertheless through the day! Let's go!

BOLD ACTIONS

_____

_____

_____

_____

_____

_____

_____

_____

_____

_____

_____

BOLD ACTIONS

_____

_____

_____

_____

_____

_____

_____

_____

_____

_____

_____

_____

BOLD ACTIONS

_____

_____

_____

_____

_____

_____

_____

_____

_____

_____

_____

BOLD ACTIONS

_____

_____

_____

_____

_____

_____

_____

_____

_____

_____

_____

DAY 11

Shift in Mindset

Never be limited by other people's limited imaginations.

—Dr. Mae Jemison
American Engineer, Physician and Astronaut

To maximize your potential and fulfill God's purposes for your life, you need to partake in a necessary mindset shift. The shift in your mind does not just magically take place. You need to be a willing vessel and active participant in the transition. But even more importantly, you must know that change is necessary to improve your life and get you to where God wants you. He wants you to surrender your old ways of thinking and invest, internalize, and live by the wisdom of the Word and the lessons taught to make the subtle and/or drastic changes that will propel you to your next level in Christ.

Romans 12:2 (NIV) states, "Do not conform to the pattern of this world, but be transformed by the renewing of your mind. Then you will be able to test and approve what God's will is—his good, pleasing, and perfect will." There is a breathtaking exuberance during the transition. The newness and realness of your new life and lifestyle is a refreshing change that makes your hopes look not only possible but obtainable. Decide today that you will undergo a shift in mindset in a particular area of life where change needs to happen. Commit yourself to do all the things necessary to win. The Lord Your God will be with you every step of the way!

BOLD ACTIONS

_____

_____

_____

_____

_____

_____

_____

_____

_____

_____

_____

_____

BOLD ACTIONS

_____

_____

_____

_____

_____

_____

_____

_____

_____

_____

_____

BOLD ACTIONS

BOLD ACTIONS

_____

_____

_____

_____

_____

_____

_____

_____

_____

_____

DAY 12

Patience in Personal Growth

I've failed over and over and over again in my life, and that is why I succeed.

—Michael Jordan
American Professional Basketball Player/
Principal Owner of the Charlotte Hornets

Building your faith takes time. No one starts out with the assurance that they can accomplish or get through anything by faith. Personal growth takes time to develop, so you need to have patience. Even those who have great faith can stand to have their faith increased. Use your steady improvements and blessings in your life since salvation as motivation that God is not finished with you. God will not leave you hanging! Has He yet? When you received Christ as your personal Savior, that sealed the deal. You just need to do your part and stay in right standing with Him. Now is that a faith boost or what! The Bible declares, "Therefore, if anyone is in Christ, the new creation has come: The old has gone, the new is here!" (2 Corinthians 5:17 NIV) So, be blessed in the patience of your personal growth. Be bold in your Christian journey! Do not be afraid to think big and fail along the way. Enjoy all the benefits and rewards of your Christian lifestyle. Eventually, you will grow to have *Bold & Crazy Faith!*

BOLD ACTIONS

_____

_____

_____

_____

_____

_____

_____

_____

_____

_____

_____

_____

_____

BOLD ACTIONS

_____

_____

_____

_____

_____

_____

_____

_____

_____

_____

_____

_____

BOLD ACTIONS

_____

_____

_____

_____

_____

_____

_____

_____

_____

_____

_____

_____

BOLD ACTIONS

_____

_____

_____

_____

_____

_____

_____

_____

_____

_____

_____

_____

_____

DAY 13

Overcoming Fear

God places the best things in life on the other side of your maximum fear!

—Will Smith
4X Grammy Award Winner, 3X Academy
Award Winner

Do not be fearful of life or whatever you have going on right now. Begin speaking positively and pushing in the right direction regarding your circumstances and watch the power of the Holy Spirit working from within begin to make things happen. God is waiting for you! In the Bible, 2 Timothy 1:7 (AMP) states, "For God did not give us a spirit of timidity *or* cowardice *or* fear, but [He has given us a spirit] of power and of love and of sound judgment *and* personal discipline [abilities that result in a calm, well-balanced mind, and self-control]."

This is a powerful scripture to build your faith. Learn, memorize, and apply it to fit into your life like a pair of gloves fits your hands. Internalize this scripture and exercise *Bold & Crazy Faith* to conquer the intimidation tactics and snares of the enemy. Walk with the Spirit of Truth and tell Satan, **"No Fear!** I am walking in power and love over here!"** When you sense the enemy is on your trail, tell the devil that he is a liar and that your God has given you a sound mind. Choose faith over fear today. Get super excited that you have one more technique to build your faith today, so that you can live boldly and abundantly in this Christian journey!

BOLD ACTIONS

_____

_____

_____

_____

_____

_____

_____

_____

_____

_____

_____

_____

BOLD ACTIONS

_____

_____

_____

_____

_____

_____

_____

_____

_____

_____

_____

BOLD ACTIONS

_____

_____

_____

_____

_____

_____

_____

_____

_____

_____

_____

BOLD ACTIONS

_____

_____

_____

_____

_____

_____

_____

_____

_____

_____

_____

DAY 14

Living as Children of God

I believed that there was a God because I was told it by my grandmother and later by other adults. But when I found that I knew not only that there was God but that I was a child of God, when I understood that, when I comprehended that, more than that, when I internalized that, ingested that, I became courageous.

—Maya Angelou
American Poet / Civil Rights Activist / Actress

When you know that you are a child of the King, you look at life from a spiritual perspective. Furthermore, when you realize who you are and whose you are, you look at life from an entirely distinct perspective. You see things through a different lens than the world's view. A King (God) takes care of His children. He protects, provides, and prospers His children to be high-achieving and productive representatives of Him. If you know that God (Holy Spirit) is in you and you are in Him (active believer), you will have Bold & Crazy Faith, "...because greater is he that is in you, than he that is in the world" (1 John 4:4 KJV).

You need to know and live your life boldly based on the kinship you share with the creator of all things and the knowledge that your Heavenly Father's plans are for you to prosper as one of His children. You may be experiencing a valley in your life right now. Everyone does. However, valley moments should not be devastating when you believe. As a child of God, you should know that you have the favor to overcome. Know that you are a child of God and live with confidence as such. Live these truths! Rise, soar, and enjoy the Christian lifestyle you were destined to live!

BOLD ACTIONS

BOLD ACTIONS

_____

_____

_____

_____

_____

_____

_____

_____

_____

_____

_____

BOLD ACTIONS

BOLD ACTIONS

_____

_____

_____

_____

_____

_____

_____

_____

_____

_____

_____

_____

DAY 15

Gospel Music Influences

I think the amazing thing about Gospel music is that not only does it lift up the death and resurrection of our Lord, which is consistent with the gospel, but it is uniquely communicated depending upon the generation.

—**Bishop T.D. Jakes**
Pastor/Movie Producer

Listening to Gospel music provides a wonderful opportunity to learn the Word of God. When you listen to Gospel music, pay special attention to the words and scripture being used. The artist's lyrics, music, and life experiences are powerful and will stimulate you significantly to help you build your faith. If you do not like to read, Gospel music offers a brilliant opportunity to build your faith. Take advantage of the influence, power, and faith-building attributes Gospel choirs have always provided. Especially today! Everyone has access to the various genres of Gospel music, including Gospel Reggae, Gospel Hip-Hop, Gospel House, and the list goes on. They are easily accessible on YouTube, iTunes, Google, and more.

Step out and try the other genres of Gospel music. Let the harmonic arrangements of Gospel Jazz without the lyrics minister to your soul and spirit. Have fun and try a genre to which you would not normally listen. Are you ready for this surprise? Obtain a hymnal, sing, and build your faith while having an exciting time praising the Lord. "Sing a new song to the LORD! Let the whole earth sing to the LORD!" (Psalm 96:1 NLT). Build your faith today with Gospel Music Influences.

BOLD ACTIONS

_____

_____

_____

_____

_____

_____

_____

_____

_____

_____

_____

_____

BOLD ACTIONS

_____

_____

_____

_____

_____

_____

_____

_____

_____

_____

BOLD ACTIONS

_____

_____

_____

_____

_____

_____

_____

_____

_____

_____

_____

BOLD ACTIONS

_____

_____

_____

_____

_____

_____

_____

_____

_____

_____

_____

_____

DAY 16

God's Assurances

When you acknowledge God, He will go before you and make the crooked places straight.

—Joel Osteen
Pastor/New York Times Best-Selling Author

You deserve peace in your life. Everyone does. However, the world is not fair, and as a Christian, you will face challenges that show up at your front door in the form of tests from God, attacks from the enemy, and even depression because of so many different things. Do yourself a favor and learn to lean hard on God's assurances. The Apostle Paul hits the nail on the head in Romans 8:37–39 (NLT), as he lays down a strong persuasive testimony assuring God's unwavering love for us. "No, despite all these things, overwhelming victory is ours through Christ, who loved us. And I am convinced that nothing can ever separate us from God's love. Neither death nor life, neither angels nor demons, neither our fears for today nor our worries about tomorrow—not even the powers of hell can separate us from God's love. No power in the sky above or in the earth below—indeed, nothing in all creation will ever be able to separate us from the love of God that is revealed in Christ Jesus our Lord." This is one powerful testimony of the love and power of God indeed. Trust and believe the Apostle Paul as he helps you understand that nothing in the entire world—from now to eternity—can isolate you from the "love of God that is in Jesus Christ your Lord." Amen!

BOLD ACTIONS

_____

_____

_____

_____

_____

_____

_____

_____

_____

_____

_____

BOLD ACTIONS

_____

_____

_____

_____

_____

_____

_____

_____

_____

_____

_____

_____

BOLD ACTIONS

_____

_____

_____

_____

_____

_____

_____

_____

_____

_____

_____

BOLD ACTIONS

_____

_____

_____

_____

_____

_____

_____

_____

_____

_____

DAY 17

Positive Influences and Associations

Choose people who lift you up.
—Michelle Obama
First Lady of the United States of America

Be initiative-taking in searching for positive influences and associations. Positive influences are people, places, and things that align with your values, morals, and ethics and can be considered positive reinforcements to living righteously. Start by recognizing and connecting with positive influences and associations already in your space. At the same time, ask God to arrange influences that are great for you and pleasing to Him. Positive associations are individuals and groups who you need to be associated with to add value to your life by promoting growth, development, accountability, and motivation to live righteously. Proverbs

27:17 (NIV) states, "As iron sharpens iron, so one person sharpens another." Having positive influences and associations in your life will help you build your faith through the edification and experiences of others. Positive influences and associations breathe life into you and assist you as you press on for the prize and press on to living your best life now!

BOLD ACTIONS

_____

_____

_____

_____

_____

_____

_____

_____

_____

_____

_____

BOLD ACTIONS

_____

_____

_____

_____

_____

_____

_____

_____

_____

_____

_____

_____

BOLD ACTIONS

_____

_____

_____

_____

_____

_____

_____

_____

_____

_____

_____

_____

BOLD ACTIONS

_____

_____

_____

_____

_____

_____

_____

_____

_____

_____

DAY 18

Meditating in the Spirit

Knowing that stillness is the space where all creative expression, peace, light, and love come to be is a powerfully energizing, yet calming experience.

—Oprah Winfrey
Golden Globe-Winning & Academy Award-Nominated American Producer/Actress

Find a quiet space and close your eyes. Make connecting with God and attaining peace your primary objective today. Fix your mind on Jesus and focus on godly things. Think deeply about your life and the things you want and do not want in your life. Be conscious and intentional. Expect the favor of God to deliver the results you are seeking during your meditation and in your life. Philippians 4:8 (NKJV) declares,

"Finally, brethren, whatever things are true, whatever things *are* noble, whatever things *are* just, whatever things *are* pure, whatever things *are* lovely, whatever things *are* of good report, if *there is* any virtue and if *there is* anything praiseworthy—meditate on these things."

Meditate on the names of God. Jesus is your Lily of the Valley. Thank Him today for being your Bright and Morning Star. Worship Him quietly this morning for being the Chief Cornerstone. Adore God, for He is the Beautiful Rose of Sharon. Meditating in the spirit is a beautiful thing. Use this time today to meditate deeply on the beauty and the splendor of everything godly. Be blessed!

BOLD ACTIONS

_____

_____

_____

_____

_____

_____

_____

_____

_____

_____

_____

_____

BOLD ACTIONS

_____

_____

_____

_____

_____

_____

_____

_____

_____

_____

BOLD ACTIONS

———————————————————————

———————————————————————

———————————————————————

———————————————————————

———————————————————————

———————————————————————

———————————————————————

———————————————————————

———————————————————————

———————————————————————

———————————————————————

BOLD ACTIONS

_____

_____

_____

_____

_____

_____

_____

_____

_____

_____

_____

DAY 19

Christian Fellowship

If you limit worship to where you are, the minute you leave that place of worship, you will leave your attitude of worship behind like a crumpled-up church bulletin.

—Dr. Tony Evans
Pastor/Best-Selling Author

Build your faith by attending and becoming a member of a Christian fellowship or church. One of the benefits of Christian fellowship is you receive encouragement from other believers. It allows you to be a part of worship and corporate prayer. Additionally, within the various ministries of a Christian fellowship, long-lasting friendships are sometimes formed and cultivated. These relationships with your brothers and sisters in Christ are beneficial, as they meet your social needs and influence your spiritual growth.

They, too, have experienced and are experiencing the highs and lows we all have in common. True, your help comes from the Lord, but it also comes from good brothers and sisters who will help you and support you as your faith continues to grow. Galatians 6:10 (NIV) says, "Therefore, as we have opportunity, let us do good to all people, especially to those who belong to the family of believers." Consider becoming a member of a Christian fellowship that teaches and follows the Word of God.

Ask God to lead you to the place He wants you to join, connect, learn, grow, and serve with other believers in Christ. If you are already a part of a fellowship, ask God today to use you in the capacity that will serve His kingdom best.

BOLD ACTIONS

BOLD ACTIONS

_____

_____

_____

_____

_____

_____

_____

_____

_____

_____

_____

_____

BOLD ACTIONS

_____

_____

_____

_____

_____

_____

_____

_____

_____

_____

_____

_____

BOLD ACTIONS

_____

_____

_____

_____

_____

_____

_____

_____

_____

_____

_____

_____

_____

DAY 20

Paul, Barnabas, and Timothy Model

We are a sum total of what we have learned from all who have taught us, both great and small.

—Miles Monroe
Pastor / Best-Selling Author / Business Consultant

Implement the Paul, Barnabas, and Timothy principle into your life to enhance your Christian lifestyle. To live by this principle, you need three specific types of people in your life. The first is a person speaking into you. Second, you need a person walking along with you. Third, you need someone in whom you are investing.

Paul is someone who mentors, advises, and guides you. This is the person who takes you under their wing and shows you what the Christian lifestyle is all about. They are authen-

117

tic followers of Christ and display that they are worthy to be modeled because of their love for Christ, godliness, and the fruit they are producing. The person who represents Paul in your life will usually be older and significantly more experienced than you. Their understanding of the Word of God and Christian affairs will qualify them to offer their knowledge and wisdom for your growth, development, and overall well-being. Are you seeking those who have come into the faith behind you to assist and influence their spiritual growth?

Barnabas is someone you consider a friend in the faith. You will see this person as a peer and carry a mutual respect as you grow and learn more about the faith together. Your Barnabas could be your prayer partner, Bible study classmate, or a member who joined the church when you did. This person can be a coworker you go to lunch with and enjoy speaking to about the goodness of God together. You genuinely want the best for each other. The spirit behind this type of relationship is that you cry and rise together. The two of you support, motivate, and hold each other accountable for living your best lives in Christ. Are you looking to cultivate relationships with other Christians to support, serve, and grow together in Christ?

Timothy is someone you disciple and lead in the right direction in their faith. A Timothy is thirsty, anxious, and impressionable enough to learn and know more about the things of God. This person clearly sees you as someone to be respected and, over time, with your direction and their perseverance, should become a great candidate to be a Barnabas and Paul in their own right.

Are you intentionally seeking out those who have come before you to assist in your spiritual growth? Having a Paul, Barnabas, and Timothy in your life will enhance your faith considerably as you gain from the uniqueness of each relationship. Begin to implement this principle to increase your boldness and enhance your life today. "But mostly, show them all this by doing it yourself, incorruptible in your teaching, your words solid and sane. Then anyone who is dead set against us, when he finds nothing weird or misguided, might eventually come around" (Titus 2:7–8 MSG).

BOLD ACTIONS

_____

_____

_____

_____

_____

_____

_____

_____

_____

_____

_____

_____

BOLD ACTIONS

_____

_____

_____

_____

_____

_____

_____

_____

_____

_____

_____

_____

BOLD ACTIONS

_____

_____

_____

_____

_____

_____

_____

_____

_____

_____

_____

BOLD ACTIONS

_____

_____

_____

_____

_____

_____

_____

_____

_____

_____

_____

BOLD ACTIONS

_____

_____

_____

_____

_____

_____

_____

_____

_____

_____

DAY 21

Faith Beyond Senses

These kinds of things don't really take the doctors, they don't really take myself. It pretty much boils down to one thing, and I think that's faith. It boils down to that. Coming from a family that has a lot of it, I'm definitely willing to take that challenge.

—**Tua Tagovailoa**
All-American Quarterback and National Champion, University of Alabama/Miami Dolphins

The five human senses are commonly known as sight, hearing, touch, smell, and taste. They send information to the brain about our environment. An argument could be made about what the most important sense is, which is relative. But let me tell you how meaningful faith is in the life of a believer and how it trumps the human

125

senses. First, having faith means not relying on any of these senses to believe that something is real. You may ask, "How do you know it's there if you cannot see it, or how do you know it's the truth if you did not hear it?" Well, faith itself goes beyond your senses. Yes! And every Christian needs faith beyond the senses to experience the abundance God has for you. You need faith beyond your senses to reach a higher level of spiritual maturity.

Sometimes you know things beyond any doubt. You may not even be able to put your finger on why you know—you just do. When you have faith beyond your senses, you can feel it in your bones. Can you see, hear, touch, smell or taste it? No. But you will know it in the core of your being. Meditate on this! It is a beautiful thing to behold and witness as it unfolds. The rewards are tremendous, and the value added to your life is indescribable. Just imagine if you could record the results of every accomplishment you will make in your life, stemming from the domino effect that happens when you are propelled into your next level of faith because you have faith beyond your senses. Your boldness in the faith will give you the victory again and again!

BOLD ACTIONS

_____

_____

_____

_____

_____

_____

_____

_____

_____

_____

_____

_____

BOLD ACTIONS

_____

_____

_____

_____

_____

_____

_____

_____

_____

_____

_____

_____

BOLD ACTIONS

_____

_____

_____

_____

_____

_____

_____

_____

_____

_____

_____

BOLD ACTIONS

_____

_____

_____

_____

_____

_____

_____

_____

_____

_____

_____

_____

DAY 22

Receiving God's Guidance

When I was taught truth, that's when I got my freedom.

—Kirk Franklin
Grammy Award-Winning Gospel Artist/
Author

A s you think about today's meditation, free yourself from the guilt of falling short in receiving or asking God for His guidance daily. You may even know in the inner depths of your heart that following God's guidance is the best thing, but life gets in the way. It is ok. Start today. Make a conscious decision not to go at things alone any longer. No more making your decisions on your own without checking in with the Lord, your Bright and Morning Star. Today and every day, be determined and declare, "Your Word is a lamp to guide my feet and a light for my path"

(Psalm 119:105 NLT).

When you find yourself stressed, overwhelmed, or lost, pause for a moment to come up for fresh air. You will realize that things are sometimes moving much too fast to even think clearly. Wisdom will teach you that no matter how fast the train of life is going, things always work out better when you receive God's guidance. His guidance for your life cannot be spelled out any clearer than in Proverbs 3:1–4 (NIV). Meditate on this:

> My son, do not forget my teaching, but keep my commands in your heart, for they will prolong your life many years and bring you peace and prosperity. Let love and faithfulness never leave you; bind them around your neck, write them on the tablet of your heart. Then you will win favor and a good name in the sight of God and man.

God is all-knowing. He knows the direction and paths that will lead you to the destinations He has designed and desired for your life. Remember, follow God today and every day!

BOLD ACTIONS

_____

_____

_____

_____

_____

_____

_____

_____

_____

_____

_____

_____

_____

BOLD ACTIONS

BOLD ACTIONS

_____

_____

_____

_____

_____

_____

_____

_____

_____

_____

_____

_____

BOLD ACTIONS

_____

_____

_____

_____

_____

_____

_____

_____

_____

_____

_____

_____

DAY 23

Praying in the Spirit

Anything you pray for; you need to prepare for.
—DeVon Franklin
Award-Winning Film Producer / New York
Times Best-Selling Author / Renowned
Preacher

What would you think if you knew that God flat out told you to help someone? Now, this is not one of those thoughts that you act upon because you know that God would be pleased if you helped someone because it was the right thing to do or because you had the means to help. When you pray, the Holy Spirit will intercede for you to give insight on what to pray to help someone else. Before you pray today and always, make sure your mind is clear. Try to block out anything that will hinder your thoughts during your prayer. Take a moment to come to God in the name of Jesus and ask that for which you should be praying. Pray for wisdom. James 1:5 (NASB) says, "But if any of you lacks wisdom, let him ask of God, who gives to all generously and without reproach, and it will be given to him."

Think deeply while asking God what He wants you to pray about according to His will. Romans 8:26–27 (ESV) says, "Likewise the Spirit helps us in our weakness. For we do not know what to pray for as we ought, but the Spirit himself intercedes for us with groanings too deep for words. And he who searches hearts knows what is the mind of the Spirit, because the Spirit intercedes for the saints according to the will of God."

Submit to God and Jesus Christ before and during your prayer, and the Holy Spirit will testify to himself in your prayers and other believers praying with you. This is certainly a challenge, and you may feel that you miss the mark in attempting to hear the Holy Spirit sometimes; however, do not worry and do not give up. Remember, growth and development happen over time. You will get better. Praying with the help of the Holy Spirit is something to get excited about! You will find that prayer guided by the Holy Spirit is one of the most beautiful, liberating, and effective actions you can take in your life as a Christian.

BOLD ACTIONS

_____

_____

_____

_____

_____

_____

_____

_____

_____

_____

_____

_____

BOLD ACTIONS

_____

_____

_____

_____

_____

_____

_____

_____

_____

_____

_____

BOLD ACTIONS

_____

_____

_____

_____

_____

_____

_____

_____

_____

_____

_____

_____

_____

BOLD ACTIONS

_____

_____

_____

_____

_____

_____

_____

_____

_____

_____

_____

_____

DAY 24

Reading Great Books

Books are a form of political action. Books are knowledge. Books are reflection. Books change your mind.

—Toni Morrison
Nobel Prize and Pulitzer Prize-Winning
Novelist/ Professor

Much can be said about the inspiration that comes from reading a great book. One thing is certain, books have been around since the beginning of time. And, of course, the Bible is known as the original good book. It does not get any better than the Bible when it comes to reading great books. The Bible covers all the areas in our lives and will provide wisdom, guidance, and understanding. But let us shift gears and talk about various kinds of books. There are terrific books on self-help, affirmations, motivation, inspiration, health, fitness, dietary, careers, and more. The definition of the word "book" in the Merriam-Webster dictionary is *something that yields knowledge or understanding*. A great book will do just that.

If you are seeking knowledge and under-standing, select a great book that will give you the knowledge and understanding you need to give yourself the best opportunity to capitalize on the opportunities that will come. Reading great books will also provide the motivation and encouragement needed to step out with confi-dence as you feel that you have the instructions to complete your assignments. It is like refer-ring to the owner's manual in a car. You may not know much about cars or how they work, but your owner's manual will provide the knowl-edge and understanding of the location and operation of your car's controls; a schedule and description of maintenance requirements, part numbers, and specific troubleshooting guidance to assist in helping you detect specific issues with your vehicle.

Let the authorities (authors) in any area provide the expertise to give you the excitement you need to be effective in your life and the lives of others. Be encouraged today by reading a great book that will thrust you into fulfilling your heart's desire and help you live your best life now.

BOLD ACTIONS

_____

_____

_____

_____

_____

_____

_____

_____

_____

_____

_____

_____

_____

BOLD ACTIONS

_____

_____

_____

_____

_____

_____

_____

_____

_____

_____

_____

_____

BOLD ACTIONS

_____

_____

_____

_____

_____

_____

_____

_____

_____

_____

_____

BOLD ACTIONS

BOLD ACTIONS

_____

_____

_____

_____

_____

_____

_____

_____

_____

_____

_____

DAY 25

Returning to Your Foundation

All things work together for good, for those who have the Lord and are called according to His purpose. So, I have foundations and He is my rock I keep going back to.

—Angela Bassett
Academy Award Nominated American
Actress/Director

You cannot have Bold & Crazy Faith from the outset. No…you cannot! Building your faith is foundational! Your foundation in the faith is what you stand on, build from, and use to grow to have Bold & Crazy Faith. Sometimes it is wise to go back to your foundation to understand the essentials of how things came to be and even why you arrived at a certain place in your Christian journey. Returning to your foundation can help you make sense of your status and support you in your quest toward your future. Often in the various arenas in life, we rise to a point where we mostly understand the complexities more than we understand the basics or foundational things that hold things and keep them together.

The foundation cannot be overlooked, as it is the key ingredient. It is like making a pot of gumbo without the roux, which is the foundational ingredient used to make this delicious dish. Sure, the onions, celery, sausage, okra, seafood, seasonings, and other ingredients are equally important; however, they are added and build from the roux and are the complexities that make the dish rich, thick, and complete. So, we need to go back to the beginning of what we learned about our faith.

The foundational and important aspects of the Christian faith should be revisited. For instance, "In the beginning was the Word, and the Word was with God, and the Word was God" (John 1:1 NIV). As a Christian, you need to know you believe in the Trinity, which is God in three Persons (God the Father, God the Son, and God the Holy Spirit). It is good to remember that God made the ultimate sacrifice by giving His only son (Jesus). It is good to read the Ten Commandments and ask the tough question, "Am I living according to these commands?" Returning to the roots of your faith is powerful and will undoubtedly place you and keep you on the right track and strengthen your walk today.

BOLD ACTIONS

_____

_____

_____

_____

_____

_____

_____

_____

_____

_____

_____

BOLD ACTIONS

_____

_____

_____

_____

_____

_____

_____

_____

_____

_____

_____

_____

_____

BOLD ACTIONS

_____

_____

_____

_____

_____

_____

_____

_____

_____

_____

_____

_____

_____

BOLD ACTIONS

_____

_____

_____

_____

_____

_____

_____

_____

_____

_____

_____

_____

_____

BOLD ACTIONS

_____

_____

_____

_____

_____

_____

_____

_____

_____

_____

_____

_____

DAY 26

Honoring Your Covenant

*I attribute my talent and my success to God,
but I believe that the only way you can manifest
what He has ordained for you is by being close
to Him and by making it happen. But we have to
stay close to Him in order to be an image of Him.*

—Nia Long
American Actress

To get the most out of your relationship with
God and improve the quality of your Christian life, honor your relationship with God. As a
Christian, you should have a special, unique, and
intimate relationship with God that has a pattern
and understanding where the two of you have
made a commitment to each other. In Genesis
17:7 (NIV), God said to Abram (later known as
Abraham), "I will establish my covenant as an
everlasting covenant between me and you and

your descendants after you for the generations to come, to be your God and the God of your descendants after you."

Your covenant with God can be a special thing, time, place, or method of communication that you and God have come to an agreement on. It can be honoring a meeting in your prayer closet on the first day of every month to check in with Him to receive direction and instruction on what He plans for you to do in the month to follow. Or your covenant with God may be a promise and agreement that you made with Him, to never go to bed angry after a disagreement without attempting reconciliation or compromise.

If you do not feel that you have an intimate relationship with God or find challenges hearing from Him clearly, start today by petitioning God to reveal Himself to you through the Spirit. Ask and declare that you want to meet and spend time with Him on a regular and reoccurring basis. Have you repented in areas of your life but find yourself continually repeating the sin even though you acknowledged the sin and asked God for forgiveness? If this is your situation, I implore you to start there. Repent and ask God for His help to deliver and heal you in this area of your life. Tell God that you do not want to indulge in this area any longer and trust that He will deliver you. Let God know today, upon His deliverance, you will give Him the honor, glory and praise and will be forever grateful to Him. Remember that your covenant with God is the understanding that He delivered on your request, and you will deliver on your Word to honor, glorify, and praise Him for showing up and delivering you from sin. Remember your covenant is between only you and God. Honor your covenant with God today!

BOLD ACTIONS

_____

_____

_____

_____

_____

_____

_____

_____

_____

_____

_____

_____

_____

BOLD ACTIONS

_____

_____

_____

_____

_____

_____

_____

_____

_____

_____

_____

_____

_____

BOLD ACTIONS

_____

_____

_____

_____

_____

_____

_____

_____

_____

_____

_____

BOLD ACTIONS

_____

_____

_____

_____

_____

_____

_____

_____

_____

_____

_____

_____

BOLD ACTIONS

_____

_____

_____

_____

_____

_____

_____

_____

_____

_____

_____

_____

DAY 27

Sacrifice

God didn't give you the strength to get back on your feet so that you can run back to the same things that knocked you down.

—Bishop Marvin Sapp
Pastor/Stellar Award-Winning Gospel Artist

Every day should be a day of sacrifice. Sacrifice is pleasing to God. When you deny your fleshly desires to stand righteous and live by the values that your Heavenly Father has given you, you store up favor with God. Romans 12:1–2 (NLT) declares, "And so, dear brothers and sisters, I plead with you to give your bodies to God because of all he has done for you. Let them be a living and holy sacrifice—the kind he will find acceptable. This is truly the way to worship him. Don't copy the behavior and customs of this world, but let God transform you into a new person by changing the way you think. Then you will learn to know God's will for you, which is good and pleasing and perfect."

And in Luke 9:23 (NLT), Jesus said to the crowd, "If any of you wants to be my follower, you must give up your own way, take up your cross daily, and follow me." In other words, "sacrifice." Follow me, die to the things of the world, and take up peace, blessings, and eternal life with me. Your Heavenly Father orchestrated the ultimate sacrifice for you and me when He gave His only son to die on the cross for the remission of our sins, that we would have eternal life. So that by itself should justify the importance of exercising sacrifice in our lives. You are fearfully and wonderfully made in the image of God, and He wants you to model His behavior. Just think of how proud your Heavenly Father will be that you are modeling His ways and being purposefully molded and transformed into a new person who is pleasing to Him. Imagine how pleased He will be when He knows you are intentionally sacrificing things in your life every day because you understand this is the order intended for your life.

BOLD ACTIONS

_____

_____

_____

_____

_____

_____

_____

_____

_____

_____

_____

BOLD ACTIONS

_____

_____

_____

_____

_____

_____

_____

_____

_____

_____

_____

BOLD ACTIONS

_____

_____

_____

_____

_____

_____

_____

_____

_____

_____

_____

_____

BOLD ACTIONS

_____

_____

_____

_____

_____

_____

_____

_____

_____

_____

_____

_____

_____

DAY 28

Embracing the Setbacks

I thrive on obstacles. If I'm told that it can't be done, then I push harder.

—Issa Rae
American Actress, Writer, Director, Producer

One way to gauge your spiritual maturity is to observe for yourself how you react and handle setbacks. You may not want to believe it, but setbacks are part of God's grand plan for your life. So do not get discouraged. Matthew 6:26 (NKJV) states, "Look at the birds of the air, for they neither sow nor reap nor gather into barns; yet your Heavenly Father feeds them. Are you not of more value than they?" Setbacks can affect you in the same way that persecution does in the life of every believer. They may throw you off course briefly, but you should realize over time that they come with the territory.

Setbacks help you to learn who you are in Christ. They make you draw from your tools and resources as a Christian, such as fasting, prayer, devotion, and worship. Setbacks will drive you to seek God and draw closer to Him for guidance, instruction, and protection. Setbacks will also help you understand the enemy and the power that you need to overcome his deception. Let's face it, without setbacks, so many people would not come to believe as strongly as they do. Some things just cannot be done on your own without the help of your Everlasting Father. You will witness on occasion that if it had not been for the everlasting arms of your Lord and Savior Jesus Christ, things would look quite different for you right now. So, thank God that the setbacks in your life have allowed you to be a personal witness with an incredible testimony of the supernatural power of the Almighty God.

BOLD ACTIONS

_____

_____

_____

_____

_____

_____

_____

_____

_____

_____

_____

BOLD ACTIONS

_____

_____

_____

_____

_____

_____

_____

_____

_____

_____

_____

_____

BOLD ACTIONS

_____

_____

_____

_____

_____

_____

_____

_____

_____

_____

_____

BOLD ACTIONS

_____

_____

_____

_____

_____

_____

_____

_____

_____

_____

_____

DAY 29

Removing the Confusion

What I'm not confused about is the world needing much more love, no hate, no prejudice, no bigotry, and more unity, peace and understanding. Period.

—Stevie Wonder
American Singer/Songwriter/Multi-instrumentalist

You will find that you cannot put a price on the effects of peace in your life. Therefore, you should remove all the confusion in your life at all costs. Satan is the author of confusion. To that end, you want to avoid Satan and his devices that are meant to cause confusion in your life. Understand this. Satan tried to confuse Jesus, so you know that he will try to confuse you. Recognize the approach Satan used with Jesus in Matthew 4, as he will invariably attempt a similar approach to confuse you.Observe Jesus' response very closely, as your response to Satan should model His boldness and knowledge of the Word:

> Then Jesus was led up by the Spirit into the wilderness to be tempted by the devil. And after fasting forty days and forty nights, he was hungry. And the tempter came and said to him, "If you are the Son of God, command these stones to become loaves of bread." But he answered, "It is written, "'Man shall not live by bread alone, but by every word that comes from the mouth of God.'" (Matthew 4:1-4 ESV)

The bible says, we should be "looking unto Jesus, the author and finisher of our faith" (Hebrews 12:2 NKJV). For this reason, we should place our focus on Him in the form of the Holy Spirit today, as He is our teacher, Wonderful Counselor, and Prince of Peace. Steer clear from confusion and destruction and run to the fruit of the Spirit—love, joy, peace, understanding, self-control, gentleness, and kindness. Today, do not take these blessings from the Lord for granted, for you have them in your life by His grace and mercy. Thank God that you are clothed and in your right mind, that His thoughts for you are good thoughts, and that you have a Heavenly

Father who has considered you in His plans before you were conceived in your mother's womb. Praise God that His plans for you are not just plans of mediocrity, but they are good plans to prosper you to have life more abundantly. Now that is something to be excited about today. Hallelujah!

BOLD ACTIONS

_____

_____

_____

_____

_____

_____

_____

_____

_____

_____

BOLD ACTIONS

_____

_____

_____

_____

_____

_____

_____

_____

_____

_____

_____

_____

_____

BOLD ACTIONS

_____

_____

_____

_____

_____

_____

_____

_____

_____

_____

_____

_____

BOLD ACTIONS

BOLD ACTIONS

_____

_____

_____

_____

_____

_____

_____

_____

_____

_____

_____

_____

DAY 30

Living a Life of Obedience

Obedience to God is the pathway to the life you really want to live.

—Joyce Meyer
American Charismatic Christian Author /
Speaker

Living a life of obedience to God is quite a challenge, to say the least. Most people do not like to be told what to do. In fact, most of us like to have our cake and eat it too. That is the American way. To that end, let us meditate on what the Word says about obedience: "Do not merely listen to the word, and so deceive yourselves. Do what it says" (James 1:22 NIV). The Word is clear on doing what the Word of God says. Even more, the Word is for your instruction, but do not place too much pressure on yourself if you fail in your journey to living a life of obedience. Sure, you can be disappointed that you missed the mark; however, understand that you will get better with time. There is still promise.

The Apostle Paul makes it clear in Hebrews 4:12 (NIV), "For the word of God is alive and active. Sharper than any double-edged sword, it penetrates even to dividing soul and spirit, joints and marrow; it judges the thoughts and attitudes of the heart." When you grow in your obedience to God, you notice more increasingly that you want to live for Christ and live less of the so-called double life. Today, make a commitment to a new life of obedience to God's will and His way. Let your focus today be on your new commitment that will pay eternal dividends in heaven. Imagine God the Father commending you for listening to His words and putting them into practice. Press on to live your life for the One who will be well pleased with your commitment of obedience in Him!

BOLD ACTIONS

_____

_____

_____

_____

_____

_____

_____

_____

_____

_____

_____

BOLD ACTIONS

_____

_____

_____

_____

_____

_____

_____

_____

_____

_____

_____

_____

BOLD ACTIONS

BOLD ACTIONS

_____

_____

_____

_____

_____

_____

_____

_____

_____

_____

_____

NOTES

Day 4: Applying God's Word, https://www.christian-today.com/article/denzel.washington.i.read.the.bible.every.day/30691.htm, accessed on June 10, 2020, 7:05 p.m.

Day 5: Affirmations to Live By, https://www.merriam-webster.com/dictionary/affirmation, accessed on June 11, 2020, at 6:07 p.m.

Day 8: Decreeing and Declaring God's Word, https://www.dictionary.com/ browse/decree, accessed on June 16, 2020, at 6:58 p.m.

Day 8: Decreeing and Declaring God's Word, https://www.dictionary.com/ browse/declare, accessed on June 16, 2020, at 6:59 p.m.

Day 8: Decreeing and Declaring God's Word, https://www.biblicalinterventions.com/post/2016/11/15/what-does-decree-declare-mean, accessed on June 16, 2020, at 7:09 p.m.

Day 9: Memorizing Verses, https://www.google.com/search?gs_ssp=eJzj4tTP1TdIMTDLNTVg9OLPyMzJSSyqVEjOycwryc8DAHU5CRE&q=hillary+clinton&rlz=1C-1JZAP_enUS763US763&oq=hillary+&aqs=-chrome.1.0j46j69i57j46l2j0l2j46.11103j0j7&sourceid=chrome&ie=UTF-8, accessed on July 10, 2020, at 7:27 p.m.

Day 14: Living as Children of God, https://www.azquotes.com/quote/800029?ref=child-of-god, accessed on June 25, 2020, at 5:20 p.m.

Day 18: Meditating in the Spirit, https://mindworks.org/blog/top-10celebrities-who-meditate/, accessed on June 30, 2020, at 5:54 p.m.

Day 19: Christian Fellowship, https://www.bing.com/search?q=if+you+limit+worship+to+where+you+are+tony+evans&cvid=e98756fafe844a59aeacbd98c50f3e06&FORM=ANNTA1&PC=LCTS, accessed on July 3, 2020, at 11:38 a.m.

Day 20: Paul, Barnabas, and Timothy Model, https://www.pamelaweaver.com/how-to-live-by-the-paul-barnabas-timothy-principle/, accessed on June 24, 2020, at 5:51 p.m.

Day 21: Faith Beyond Senses, https://www.worldatlas.com/articles/whatare-the-five-senses.html, accessed on June 16, 2020, at 7:53 p.m.

Day 21: Faith Beyond Senses, https://sportsspectrum.com/sport/football/2020/01/06/qb-tua-tagovailoa-thanks-lord-savior-declares-nfl-draft/, accessed on July 8, 2020, at 7:03 p.m.

Day 23: Praying in the Spirit, http://smartandrelentless. com/top-20-inspirational-quotes-by-devon-franklin/#:~:text=Image%20source%20-%20Bet. com.%20Top%2020%20inspirational%20quotes,of%20 in%20your%20life%2C%20is%20going%20to%20die, accessed on July 9, 2020, at 10:07 p.m.

Day 24: Reading Great Books, https://www.merriam-webster.com/dictionary/book, accessed on June 6, 2020, at 6:27 a.m.

Day 24: Reading Great Books, https://www.writersdigest.com/be-inspired/toni-morrison-quotes-for-writers-and-about-writing#:~:text=%22If%20there's%20 a%20book%20that,then%20you%20must%20write%20 it.%22, accessed on July 7, 2020, at 7:06 p.m.

Day 24: Reading Great Books, https://www.writersdigest.com/be-inspired/toni-morrison-quotes-for-writers-and-aboutwriting#:~:text=%22If%20there's%20a%20 book%20that,then%20you%20must%20write%20it.%22, accessed on July 7, 2020, at 7:06 p.m.

Day 25: Returning to Your Foundation, https://www. beliefnet.com/columnists/idolchatter/2018/05/angela-bassett-found-god.html, accessed on June 30, 2020, at 6:05 p.m.

Day 29: Removing the Confusion, https://www.britannica.com/biography/Stevie-Wonder, accessed on July 3, 2020, at 6:59 p.m.

Day 29: Removing the Confusion, https://www. google.com/search?q=what+i%27m+not+confused+about+is+the+world+needs&tbm=isch&ved=2ahUKEwiQ6qTvgrvqAhX4Vd8KHZZlCn4Q2-cCegQIABAA&oq=what+i%27m+not+confused+about+is+the+world+needs&gs_lcp=CgNpb WcQDFAAWABgguwBaABwAHgAgAEAiAEAkgEAmAEAqgELZ3dzLXdpei1pbWc&sclient=img&ei=f1oEX9CuM_ir_QaWy6nwBw&bih=461&biw= 1075&rlz=1C1JZAP_enUS763US763#imgrc=yWA8Gq8hNOlvsM, accessed on July 7, 2020 at 6:51 p.m.

Day 30: Living A Life of Obedience, https://www. google.com/search?gs_ssp=eJzj4tTP1TewNCipLDFg9OLOyq9MTlXITa1MLQIAWOEHuw&q=joyce+ meyer&rlz=1C1JZAP_enUS763US763&oq=joyce+myer&aqs=chrome.1.69i 57j46j0l3j46j0.9312j1j7&sourceid=chrome&ie=UTF-8, accessed on July 10, 2020, at 7:14 p.m.

ALSO, BY DARYN CARL RAMSEY

Bold & Crazy Faith: The Inspirational

CONNECT & SHARE

If you enjoyed this book, please connect with the author, leave a review on Amazon.com, and purchase copies for loved ones.

Connect with Author Daryn Carl Ramsey:

Website: DarynCarlRamsey.com
Instagram: @daryncarlramsey
Facebook: @daryncarlramsey
Twitter: @daryncarlramsey

Made in the USA
Middletown, DE
11 February 2023

24565838R00119